" THE DARK SIDE OF THE FORCE IS A PATHWAY TO MANY ABILITIES...

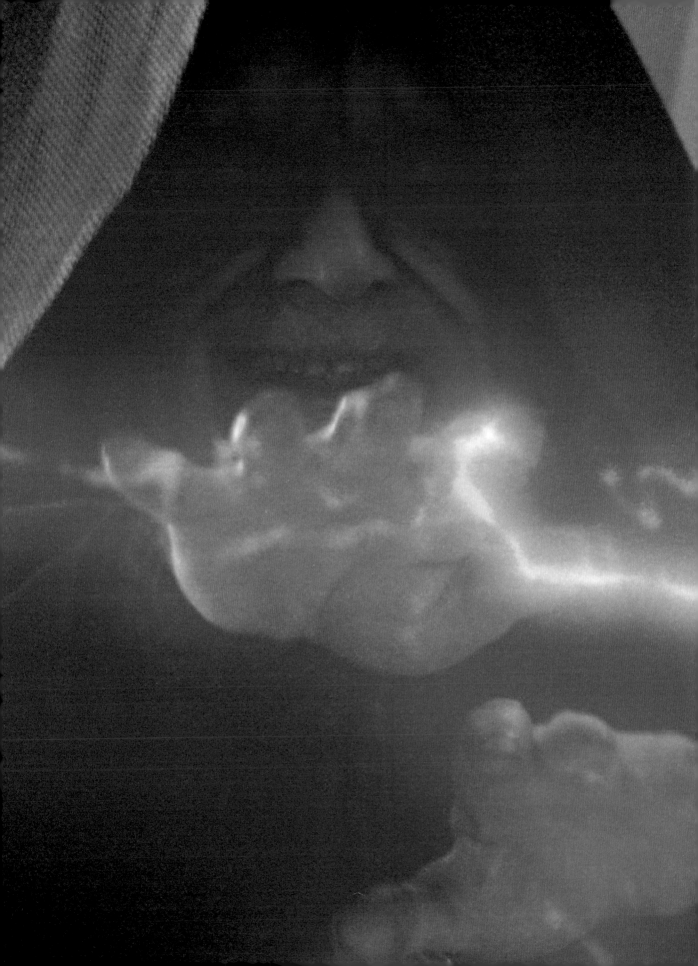

...SOME CONSIDER TO BE UNNATURAL."

STAR WARS™

BEWARE THE SITH

WRITTEN BY
SHARI LAST

CONTENTS

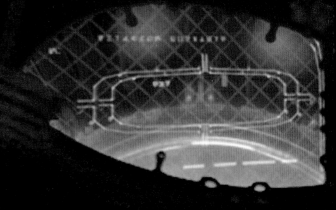

SITH SECRETS

■ The Sith guard their secrets very closely. Throughout the book, look out for Sith Secrets in special boxes like this.

According to the Rule of Two, only two Sith can exist at once, a Master and an apprentice. Darth Sidious and his apprentice, Darth Vader, have embarked on a plan to build the most ambitious and terrifying weapon the galaxy has ever seen... the Death Star.

22 BBY: BATTLE OF GEONOSIS

19 BBY: PALPATINE BECOMES EMPEROR

41 BBY: BIRTH OF ANAKIN

32 BBY: BATTLE OF NABOO

19 BBY: DARTH VADER IS CREATED

50 BBY   **40 BBY**   **30 BBY**   **20 BBY**

REPUBLIC ERA

THE CLONE WARS

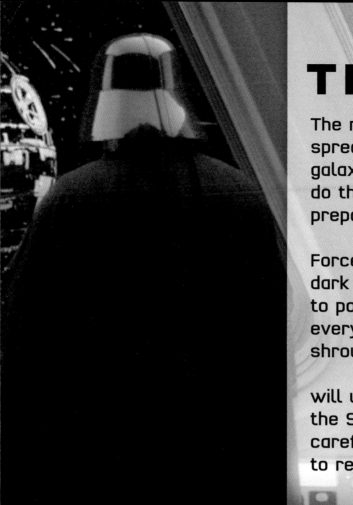

THE SITH

The mere mention of the word "Sith" spreads a ripple of fear across the galaxy. But who are the Sith? What do they want – and how far are they prepared to go to obtain it?

The Sith are an ancient group of Force-sensitive beings who study the dark side of the Force and are known to possess incredible power – but everything else about them is shrouded in secrecy.

Now, for the first time, you will uncover some of the secrets of the Sith. But beware! If you are not careful, you may find yourself unable to resist the power of the dark side...

NOTE ON DATES: Dates are fixed around the Battle of Yavin in year 0. All events prior to this are measured in terms of years Before the Battle of Yavin (BBY). Events after it are measured in terms of years After the Battle of Yavin (ABY).

0: FIRST DEATH STAR IS DESTROYED
AT BATTLE OF YAVIN

3 ABY: BATTLE OF HOTH

4 ABY: SECOND DEATH STAR IS
DESTROYED AT BATTLE OF ENDOR

10 BBY   **0**   **10 ABY**   **20 ABY**

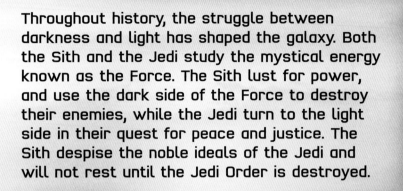

Throughout history, the struggle between darkness and light has shaped the galaxy. Both the Sith and the Jedi study the mystical energy known as the Force. The Sith lust for power, and use the dark side of the Force to destroy their enemies, while the Jedi turn to the light side in their quest for peace and justice. The Sith despise the noble ideals of the Jedi and will not rest until the Jedi Order is destroyed.

The Jedi Order was created by Force-sensitive beings who study the light side of the Force. Their honourable quest for galactic peace, however, is often undermined by the existence of the Sith and their dark motives. When the Sith re-emerge after millennia of silence, the Jedi Order has no choice: it is time for war.

ANCIENT

The Sith Order was founded by a group of wayward Jedi. Dissatisfied with the teachings of the light side, these former Jedi Knights turned to the dark side in search of greater power. The Sith have concealed their presence from the Jedi for over 1,000 years, waiting for the perfect time to make their return.

HATRED

THE DARK SIDE

Fear and mystery surround the dark side of the Force. Whispered stories and strange rumours are all that is known about the Sith and their deadly powers. The Sith rule from the shadows, using their terrible powers to shroud the galaxy in darkness and bend others to their will. There is only one way to discover all the secrets of the dark side – by joining the Sith.

TERRIFYING POWER

RUTHLESS AMBITION

SECRET TEACHINGS

UNSPEAKABLE EVIL

THE SITH CODE

Peace is a lie, there is only passion.
Through passion, I gain strength.
Through strength, I gain power.
Through power, I gain victory.
Through victory, my chains are broken.
The Force shall free me.

The Rule
OF TWO

In the past, there were many Sith. They studied the Force and grew powerful – but they also became suspicious of each other. Fighting broke out among them and the Sith Order was greatly weakened. The Rule of Two was introduced to prevent the power of the dark side from destroying the Order.

POWER HUNGRY

The Rule of Two states that there can be only one Sith Master and only one apprentice at any time. When the apprentice grows more powerful than his Master, he is to destroy him and choose an apprentice of his own. But the Rule of Two has a flaw: the Sith Code encourages passion and ambition – not loyalty. As long as the Sith exist, there will always be a brutal struggle for power.

SITH SECRETS

■ Darth Bane was a Sith Lord who lived over 1,000 years ago. He became dissatisfied with his Sith brotherhood and created his own Sith Order, in which he instituted the Rule of Two.

APPRENTICE'S APPRENTICE

Many Sith apprentices don't obey the Rule of Two and secretly take on their own apprentices. Sidious began training Darth Maul before he had destroyed his own Master, Darth Plagueis. Darth Tyranus trained Asajj Ventress and Savage Opress while he was Sidious's apprentice, and Darth Vader had a secret apprentice called Galen Marek.

EXPENDABLE APPRENTICE

Darth Tyranus is Sidious's second apprentice, but he is needed only until Sidious succeeds in turning Anakin Skywalker to the dark side. Sidious does not expect Tyranus's powers to eclipse his own, and plans to have Tyranus destroyed when the time is right.

UNWANTED APPRENTICE

Darth Sidious watched Anakin for years before the Jedi became his Sith apprentice. But Darth Vader was gravely wounded by Obi-Wan on the volcano planet Mustafar, so he now feels trapped in his armoured body. Vader is no longer the apprentice that Sidious hoped he would be.

" TWO THERE SHOULD BE. NO MORE, NO LESS. ONE TO EMBODY POWER, THE OTHER TO CRAVE IT.

DARTH BANE

SITH SELECTION

Are your Force powers exceptional? Do you care only about yourself? Is it hard to control your feelings of anger and greed? Do you think you should be more powerful than anyone else? These are some of the dark qualities Darth Sidious searches for in a new Sith apprentice.

DARTH MAUL

Raw power • Aggressive • Obedient

STRONG-MINDEDNESS: 5
LIGHTSABER SKILL: 7
FORCE SKILL: 8
RAW POWER: 9
CUNNING: 3

Darth Maul has been honing his dark side skills since he was a child. He is a talented, agile fighter and will obey his Master without question. Maul is naturally strong in the Force, but is he too confident?

DARTH TYRANUS

Ambitious • Intelligent • Remorseless

STRONG-MINDEDNESS: 7
LIGHTSABER SKILL: 10
FORCE SKILL: 7
RAW POWER:
CUNNING: 8

Former Jedi Count Dooku is arrogant and ambitious. His never-ending search for power means he will be unable to resist the temptation of the dark side. Darth Tyranus is immensely powerful, but can he defeat his former Jedi allies?

A NEW APPRENTICE
Choosing a Sith apprentice
is an important decision.
Darth Sidious considers
the personality, skills
and raw power of his
candidates so he can
choose wisely. Then he
exploits their weaknesses
and promises them what
they desire in an effort to
lure them to the dark side.

DARTH VADER

Emotional • Impatient • Open to temptation

STRONG-MINDEDNESS: 8
LIGHTSABER SKILL: 9
FORCE SKILL: 9
RAW POWER: 8
CUNNING: 5

Jedi Anakin Skywalker conceals a
growing frustration with the Jedi
Code. His troubled memories, feelings
of fear and emotional greed make him
a perfect Sith candidate. Blinded by
his own feelings, will
Anakin succumb to
the dark side?

LUKE SKYWALKER

Strong in the Force • Impulsive • Naive

STRONG-MINDEDNESS: 10
LIGHTSABER SKILL: 8
FORCE SKILL: 9
RAW POWER: 7
CUNNING: 6

Luke Skywalker is eager to
learn the truth about his
father, Anakin. Luke's
innocence might lead
him to underestimate
the power of the
dark side. Is he
strong-minded
enough to resist?

A SMILING VILLAIN

Posing as Chancellor Palpatine, Darth Sidious conceals his Sith identity for years, waiting for the right time to reveal himself. He uses his alter ego to influence the decisions of the Republic, discover the workings of the Jedi Order and seek out a new, powerful Sith apprentice.

As Emperor, Darth Sidious is in control of the entire galaxy. His appearance suggests an old, frail man – but don't be fooled! Sidious possesses almost unlimited Force powers.

Darth SIDIOUS

It has been many centuries since a Sith Lord was powerful enough to step out from the shadows. Darth Sidious spent years gathering his strength, destroying his enemies and watching his deadly plans play out. Now, as Emperor Palpatine, he has emerged from hiding and placed the galaxy under Sith control.

SITH STATS

SPECIES: HUMAN

HOMEWORLD: NABOO

BIRTHDATE: 82 BBY

HEIGHT: 1.73 M (5 FT 8 IN)

TRAINED BY: DARTH PLAGUEIS

WEAPONS: RED-BLADED LIGHTSABER

TRADEMARK: SITH LIGHTNING

BLACK ZEYD-
CLOTH ROBES
GIVE SIDIOUS
AN AIR OF
SECRECY

HIDDEN THREAT

Darth Sidious will do whatever it takes to get what he wants: he uses his immense dark side powers to manipulate, betray and murder. Sidious also uses secrecy as a weapon, concealing his face under his dark cloak to hide his true identity.

TWO MASTERS

The dark and light sides of the Force clash when Darth Sidious duels Yoda in the Senate building. Sidious battles with passion and fury, only to be matched at every blow by Yoda's calm, measured skill. Although unable to defeat Yoda, Sidious's strength forces the Jedi to flee.

19

TAKE CONTROL

Darth Sidious's alter ego Palpatine is the respected Senator of Naboo. The Sith Lord has evil plans in store for the galaxy, but he requires a lot more political power to carry them out. Sidious devises a cunning five-step strategy, designed to turn a simple Senator into an all-powerful leader. So begins his rise to power...

1. CREATE A PROBLEM

2. BECOME SUPREME CHANCELLOR

OBJECTIVE:
Create unrest in the Senate by initiating a political disturbance.

OUTCOME:
Invasion of Naboo and resulting conflict sparks fear and uncertainty in the Senate. MISSION COMPLETE.

OBJECTIVE:
Cause the Senate to lose confidence in the current Chancellor, Valorum.

OUTCOME:
Manipulated by Palpatine, Queen Amidala calls for new Senate election. Palpatine is voted Supreme Chancellor. MISSION COMPLETE.

> **Hundreds of Senators are now UNDER THE INFLUENCE of a Sith Lord.**
> **COUNT DOOKU**

3. ESTABLISH TRUST

OBJECTIVE:
Palpatine to gain the trust and support of the Senate and Jedi Order.

OUTCOME:
Palpatine is included and applauded in the Naboo celebrations.
MISSION COMPLETE.

4. GAIN EMERGENCY POWERS

OBJECTIVE:
Palpatine to increase his powers and gain more control over Senate.

OUTCOME:
Jar Jar Binks proposes the Senate give emergency powers to Palpatine.
MISSION COMPLETE.

5. JEDI COUNCIL SPY

OBJECTIVE:
Palpatine to place a spy on the Jedi Council.

OUTCOME:
Anakin Skywalker appointed as Jedi Council member.
MISSION COMPLETE.

CONSEQUENCES:

Darth Sidious is now in a prime position to be kept informed of all the happenings of the Republic. As Supreme Chancellor Palpatine, he has more power than ever before and he is able to control the actions of the Galactic Senate. But Sidious hasn't finished: he will not stop until he destroys the Jedi Order.

OFFICE OF THE CHANCELLOR

When Chancellor Palpatine discusses political matters in his office in the Senate building, no one suspects his true Sith identity. But the devious Palpatine cannot resist designing his office to hint at a darker personality. If you look closely, you'll find a surprising number of references to the Sith among the Chancellor's possessions.

CEREMONIAL OFFICE

ARMOURED CHAIR

The Chancellor's grand and airy Ceremonial Office is used for official meetings. Palpatine's Chair of Office looks ordinary, but it is built from lanthanide armour and is protected by a state-of-the-art defence shield. The arms feature a built-in comlink to summon the Red Guard.

DARK ORNAMENT

Those who have studied the teachings of the dark side will recognise this Sith Chalice. It houses sacred Korribanian incense for conducting a Sith Fire Ritual. Palpatine displays it in plain sight, confident that no one will realise its true origins.

RELICS OF THE SITH

Two ornate black vases stand by the entrance to the Private Office. Visitors never enter this room, so Palpatine has not tried to mask his sinister taste. These objects are Spirit Urns, which hold the remains of former Sith Lords, including Sidious's Master, Darth Plagueis.

KEEPING SECRETS

The Chancellor's Private Office is perfect for top-secret meetings. Palpatine uses the computer equipment in this room to communicate with his Sith apprentice and to store his plans for the Death Star project.

PRIVATE OFFICE

HIDDEN WEAPON

Four statues in the office show the Sages of Dwartii, ancient, controversial philosophers. The statue of Sistros stands just outside the Private Office, and it has a special purpose: it conceals Palpatine's lightsaber in a chamber behind its arms.

DECEPTIVE ART

An enormous, sculpted artwork hangs in an antechamber between the Ceremonial and Private Office. It depicts a battle between Jedi and Sith during the Great Hyperspace War of 5,000 BBY. Although the Jedi were victorious, if you look closely, the artwork glorifies the Sith warriors.

sith
LIGHTSABERS

The Sith possess enough Force power to battle without a lightsaber, but each new apprentice chooses his own weapon as part of his training. Sith lightsabers are powered by synthetic red crystals, which emit a strong crimson blade – reflecting the Sith's passion, bloodlust and rage.

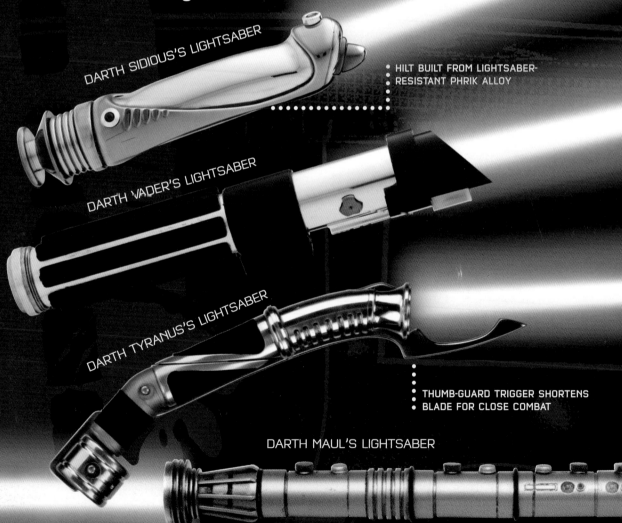

DARTH SIDIOUS'S LIGHTSABER

HILT BUILT FROM LIGHTSABER-RESISTANT PHRIK ALLOY

DARTH VADER'S LIGHTSABER

DARTH TYRANUS'S LIGHTSABER

THUMB-GUARD TRIGGER SHORTENS BLADE FOR CLOSE COMBAT

DARTH MAUL'S LIGHTSABER

Darth Sidious's ornate aurodium-plated lightsaber hilt reflects his passion for dark objects of antiquity. Its rounded form allows for fluid movement in combat.

Darth Vader's black-alloy lightsaber closely resembles the style of his Jedi weapon. To fit his mechanical hands, however, Vader's lightsaber hilt is larger than normal.

Darth Tyranus uses the same lightsaber he built when he was a Jedi. Its curved hilt is designed for precise handling. When Tyranus became a Sith, Sidious gave him a new red crystal to replace his green blade.

Darth Maul finds a single-bladed lightsaber limiting in combat. His saberstaff is perfect for attacking two opponents at once, but its size means that Maul has to be more acrobatic in battle.

OSTENTATIOUS HAT LOOKS IMPORTANT

TRADE FEDERATION SENATOR
The Trade Federation is so influential, it has its own Senate representative, Lott Dod. Dod is power-hungry and insincere.

LOTT DOD

ELABORATE ROBE BOUGHT WITH TRADE FEDERATION CREDITS

NUTE GUNRAY

TRADE FEDERATION

LEADER: NUTE GUNRAY
ALLEGIANCE: SEPARATISTS
HEADQUARTERS: TRADE FEDERATION BATTLESHIP
WEAPONS: DROID ARMY
VALUES: MONEY, POWER

COWARDLY VICEROY
The Trade Federation Viceroy, Nute Gunray, initially accepted Sith control to gain wealth and power. He revels in his new-found power, but lives in fear of Darth Sidious.

When the Neimoidians realise the extent of Sith power, they regret that they ever made a bargain with the Sith. But it is too late.

A SECRET ARMY

Following Darth Sidious's orders, the Trade Federation secretly creates a heavily armed Droid Army. They deploy the army on the planet Naboo, sparking a galactic crisis.

Pawns
of the SITH

The Trade Federation is a powerful organisation that governs trade throughout the galaxy. It has, however, become corrupt and greedy. Its Neimoidian leaders conceal their allegiance to the Sith by pretending to carry out political missions.

SITH POWERS

As a member of the Order of the Sith, you will learn to harness the power of the dark side. These powers are deadly and unpredictable – but when used correctly, they are almost unstoppable. If you are cornered by a Jedi Knight, or come face to face with a threatening bounty hunter, call on the dark side of the Force. But remember: using these powers can be extremely dangerous.

FORCE CLOUDING

CHANNEL THROUGH: Mind
SITH EXPERT: Darth Sidious can cloud the Force so completely, the Jedi remain unaware of his Sith identity.
DANGER LEVEL: Low – unless discovered!

MIND CONTROL

CHANNEL THROUGH: Mind
SITH EXPERT: Darth Tyranus can control the minds of most of his enemies –although some Jedi are able to resist.
DANGER LEVEL: Moderate

FORCE CHOKE

CHANNEL THROUGH: Hands
SITH EXPERT: Darth Vader can use the Force to strangle his victims without touching them.
DANGER LEVEL: Moderate

POWER OVER DEATH

CHANNEL THROUGH: Body and mind
SITH EXPERT: Darth Sidious uses his dark side powers to extend his life and to save Anakin from certain death.
DANGER LEVEL: High

SITH LIGHTNING

CHANNEL THROUGH: Hands
SITH EXPERT: Darth Sidious can emit intense bolts of deadly lightning for extended periods of time.
DANGER LEVEL: High

TELEKINESIS

CHANNEL THROUGH: Hands and arms
SITH EXPERT: Darth Tyranus can move extremely heavy objects with very little effort.
DANGER LEVEL: Moderate

FORBIDDEN KNOWLEDGE

CHANNEL THROUGH: Mind
SITH EXPERT: Darth Sidious claims to know the dangerous secret of immortality
DANGER LEVEL: High

WHAT HAPPENS WHEN YOU USE THE POWER OF THE DARK SIDE?

THE DARK SIDE OF the Force offers unlimited power, but harnessing that power requires a terrible sacrifice. The dark side affects its users deeply, damaging their bodies, minds and souls. And, as Anakin demonstrates when he attacks Padmé on Mustafar, it can even corrupt the most legendary Jedi hero.

UNFORGIVABLE ACTIONS
When Anakin turns to the dark side, his terrible actions corrupt his soul. Under orders to wipe out the Jedi Order, the newly named Darth Vader destroys an entire class of innocent Jedi Younglings.

PHYSICAL TRANSFORMATION

The power of the dark side is so destructive, it can permanently damage a living body. When Darth Sidious fires intense bolts of Sith lightning at Mace Windu, Sidious's eyes turn yellow and his skin wrinkles and sags. Now there is no hiding his Sith identity.

BETRAYAL

Darth Vader uses a Force choke on Padmé until she loses consciousness. He is so consumed by the dark side that he duels with Obi-Wan Kenobi, leaving his wife where she lies.

If you choose the dark side, you embark on a quest for forbidden knowledge. While you will become incredibly powerful, you will also change. First, you will fall prey to your passion. You will become selfish and greedy. Your family and friends will be afraid of you and grow distant. Eventually, all of these changes will begin to affect your physical body and it will be transformed by the dark side of the Force.

BECOMING A SITH

SENATOR PALPATINE

SUPREME CHANCELLOR

THE TRANSFORMATION

If you fully embrace the power of the dark side, your skin will become withered and pale, your eyes will grow bloodshot and your irises will turn yellow. Darth Sidious maintained his human appearance for many years, but the more he used his powers, the more they affected his body. During his years as Supreme Chancellor, he grew paler and more wrinkled, though he continued to mask his transformation in public. But after using an intense burst of Sith lightning against Mace Windu, Sidious's appearance changed dramatically, forever.

DARTH SIDIOUS

EMPEROR PALPATINE

33

Ancient ENEMY

The Jedi Order has always opposed the Sith: while the Sith revel in darkness, the Jedi seek light. As the Sith plan to start a war, the Jedi strive to keep the peace. And when the Sith attempt to oppress the galaxy, the Jedi Order stands in their way.

Important decisions are made by the Jedi Council. When Anakin Skywalker is brought before them, they are unsure whether he should be trained as a Jedi. The Council detects much fear in the young boy.

YODA

WISE LEADER
Master Yoda leads the Jedi in times of peace and war. Renowned for his wisdom, Yoda is usually able to sense Force disturbances, but the Sith can cloud his vision.

• • • • • • • • • • • • COARSE, SIMPLE ROBE
IS A SIGN OF HUMILITY

JEDI GENERALS

Sometimes, war is necessary to achieve peace. When the Sith spark the Clone Wars, Jedi Masters such as Mace Windu and Obi-Wan Kenobi charge into battle alongside the Clone Army.

OBI-WAN IS FAMOUS FOR KEEPING CALM UNDER PRESSURE

LIGHTSABER POWERED BY UNIQUE VIOLET CRYSTAL

OBI-WAN KENOBI

MACE WINDU

TROUBLE AT THE TEMPLE

After a thousand years of relative peace, the Jedi are taken by surprise when they are attacked by their own Clone Army. Although the Jedi try to resist, their Temple is destroyed and the survivors are forced into exile.

JEDI ORDER

LEADER: YODA
ALLEGIANCE: REPUBLIC
HEADQUARTERS: CORUSCANT
WEAPONS: LIGHTSABER, CLONE ARMY
VALUES: JUSTICE, PEACE, LOYALTY, HONOUR

TOUGH, LEATHER COMBAT BOOTS

SITH ARTEFACTS

The Sith treasure ancient objects that reflect their grand history. Even though they usually live in hiding, they surround themselves with powerful artefacts and ancient treasures. These items remind the Sith of their dark side identity, but appear harmless to others. The Sith also make use of sophisticated equipment on their evil missions. Beware!

3

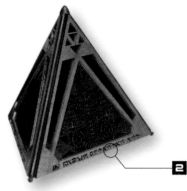

2

4

1

5

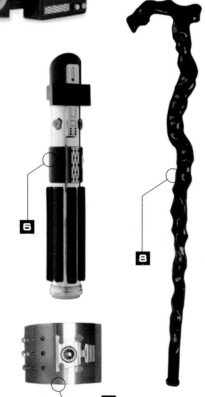

9

6

8

7

KEY

1. ELECTROBINOCULARS with target locator for tracking enemies.

2. HOLOCRON stores ancient Sith data, which can be accessed only through use of the Force.

3. Compact, undetectable TRACER BEACON for tracking enemies.

4. Synthetic LIGHTSABER CRYSTAL to power Sith lightsabers.

5. FUNCTION CONTROL BELT regulates life-supporting armour and mask. Used by Darth Vader.

6. LIGHTSABER for use during duels.

7. WRIST LINK for remote control of probe droids. Also able to arm traps and detonate bombs.

8. BLACK CANE gives its owner the appearance of weakness. Darth Sidious carries it when he is Emperor.

9. Statue of the ancient Dwartii Sage BRAATA, who encouraged the study of the dark side.

10. HOLOGRAM WATCH for communicating with Sith Master via hologram.

11. SITH CHALICE holds rare Korribanian incense, which is used in Sith rituals.

12. Compact, desk-mounted HOLOPROJECTOR for displaying hologram transmissions.

13. FORCE DISPERSER for concealing a Sith presence in the Force. Sidious places this on his desk in the Chancellor's office.

14. MEDICAL KIT contains life-saving potions and equipment.

15. Ornate SPIRIT URN to hold objects of importance.

16. Ancient BANE STATUE rotates to identify nearby Force users.

FIERCE WARRIOR

Darth Maul's character was forged from an early age to be cruel. Darth Sidious spotted useful potential in Maul when he was an infant and trained him secretly in the dark side. The young Sith learned to have no mercy and show no fear.

Darth MAUL

Thanks to his mastery of martial arts and his deadly saberstaff, Darth Maul is a fearsome opponent. His brief duel with Qui-Gon on Tatooine further fans the flames of his hatred and he lusts to finish off the Jedi Master.

After millennia of silence, the Sith reemerge with the appearance of Darth Maul on Tatooine. Strong in the Force and skillful with a lightsaber, this mysterious Sith is a dangerous dark side warrior.

SITH STATS

SPECIES: ZABRAK
HOMEWORLD: DATHOMIR
BIRTHDATE: 54 BBY
HEIGHT: 1.75 M (5 FT 9 IN)
TRAINED BY: DARTH SIDIOUS
WEAPONS: DOUBLE-BLADED RED LIGHTSABER (SABERSTAFF)
TRADEMARK: MARTIAL ARTS

BLACK AND RED
TATTOOS COVER
ENTIRE BODY

YELLOW IRIS

DEDICATED ZABRAK

As a Zabrak, Maul is a humanoid creature with horns and distinctive facial tattoos particular to the Nightbrothers clan of Dathomir. A proud and confident species, Zabraks are known for their single-mindedness, which Maul brings to his study of the dark side.

PRIDE BEFORE A FALL

Maul is a master of lightsaber combat, but his overconfidence is his downfall. When he duels two Jedi Knights on Naboo, the Sith defeats Qui-Gon Jinn, only to fall to Qui-Gon's Padawan, Obi-Wan Kenobi.

WHAT HAPPENS WHEN ONE SITH TAKES ON TWO JEDI?

DARTH MAUL IS highly skilled and well trained. He does not hesitate to engage two Jedi in battle in the Theed Generator Complex. Maul demonstrates his agility and lightsaber prowess during the duel, although he is unable to defeat both Jedi at once. But Maul proves how deadly he is by separating his opponents and taking them on one at a time.

BATTLE PLAN
Darth Maul is confident that he can defeat both Jedi with his double-bladed lightsaber. He uses his Force skills to sense where his opponents will strike next.

DIVIDE AND CONQUER

During the battle, Darth Maul forces his opponents through a security hallway. When the laser doors separate Qui-Gon from Obi-Wan, Maul knows it's the perfect time to strike. Despite Qui-Gon's skill, Maul's strength overwhelms him and the noble Jedi is defeated.

DOWNFALL

Enraged by the murder of his Master, Obi-Wan charges at Darth Maul. Although Obi-Wan's anger almost leads to his downfall, the Jedi summons all of his Force strength for a final attack on Maul, eventually defeating the Sith.

DARTH MAUL: LIGHTSABER COMBAT

Wielding a double-bladed saberstaff means that Darth Maul must choose his battle style carefully. The deadly Sith apprentice has developed his own unique form of lightsaber combat, which takes advantage of his strength and agility – and makes him almost unbeatable.

Darth Maul trained in the lightsaber combat form Juyo, which allows him to use his natural athletic abilities in battle. Using martial arts during a duel gives Maul the advantage of surprise. He also studies the style Niman, which focuses on balance, specifically for combat with dual blades.

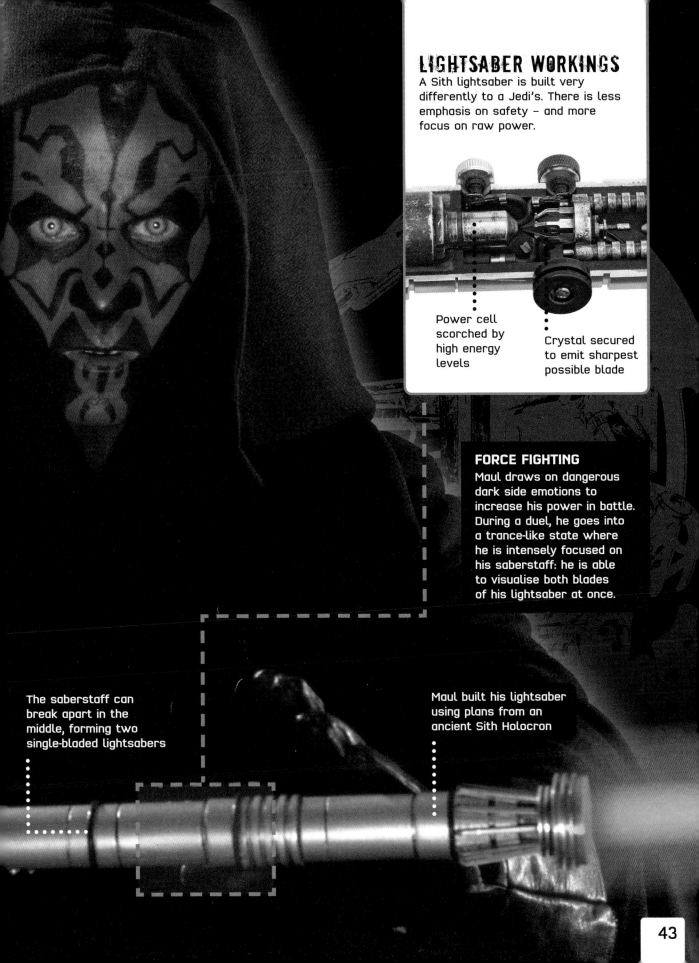

LIGHTSABER WORKINGS

A Sith lightsaber is built very differently to a Jedi's. There is less emphasis on safety – and more focus on raw power.

Power cell scorched by high energy levels

Crystal secured to emit sharpest possible blade

FORCE FIGHTING

Maul draws on dangerous dark side emotions to increase his power in battle. During a duel, he goes into a trance-like state where he is intensely focused on his saberstaff: he is able to visualise both blades of his lightsaber at once.

The saberstaff can break apart in the middle, forming two single-bladed lightsabers

Maul built his lightsaber using plans from an ancient Sith Holocron

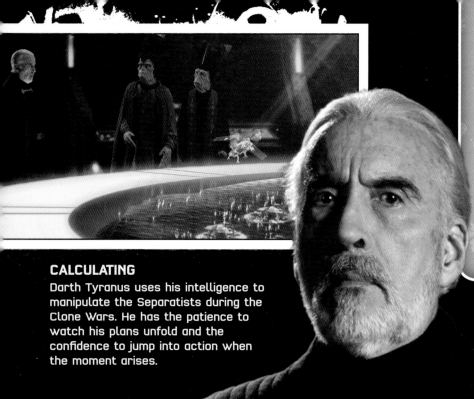

SITH STATS

SPECIES: HUMAN
HOMEWORLD: SERENNO
BIRTHDATE: 102 BBY
HEIGHT: 1.93 M (6 FT 4 IN)
TRAINED BY: DARTH SIDIOUS
WEAPONS: CURVED RED-BLADED LIGHTSABER
TRADEMARK: LIGHTSABER PROWESS

CALCULATING

Darth Tyranus uses his intelligence to manipulate the Separatists during the Clone Wars. He has the patience to watch his plans unfold and the confidence to jump into action when the moment arises.

CAPE IN THE ANCIENT STYLE OF SERENNO ROYALTY

MASTER OF LIGHTSABER COMBAT FORM II, MAKASHI

SUPERIORITY COMPLEX

Formerly known as Count Dooku, Tyranus believes he is smarter and more powerful than almost everyone else. His formidable lightsaber skills make him even more arrogant, but Tyranus should remember that pride often comes before a fall.

SEARCHING FOR POWER

Count Dooku sincerely wants to combat corruption in the Senate, but his quest has led him down a path to the dark side. Dooku used to be a Jedi Master, but his ambition was his downfall. He joined the Sith and became Darth Tyranus because the dark side offered him more power.

Despite his deadly lightsaber skills, Darth Tyranus is no match for his former Master Yoda when they duel on Geonosis.

Darth
TYRANUS

As leader of the Separatists, Darth Tyranus answers to no one but his Sith Master, Darth Sidious. Tyranus implements his master's evil plans, spreading war across the galaxy, confident that he is Sidious's only trusted servant. But Tyranus will soon learn never to trust a Sith.

LASER CANNON ABLE TO DESTROY AN ASTEROID

TIE ADVANCED X1
- **SIZE** 9.2 m (30 ft) long
- **MAX ACCELERATION** 4,150 G
- **CAPACITY** 1 pilot
- **WEAPONS** 2 laser cannons

BENT SOLAR ARRAY WINGS

DARTH VADER

SUPER STAR DESTROYER, *EXECUTOR*
- **SIZE** 19,000 m (62,336 ft) long
- **MAX ACCELERATION** 1,230 G
- **CAPACITY** 279,144 crew, 38,000 passengers
- **WEAPONS** 5,000 turbolaser and ion cannons, 250 concussion missile batteries, 40 tractor beam projectors

IMPOSING COMMAND TOWER

HANGAR BAY CAN HOLD THOUSANDS OF STARFIGHTERS

SITH INFILTRATOR, *SCIMITAR*
- **SIZE** 26.5 m (87 ft) long
- **MAX ACCELERATION** 3,730 G
- **CAPACITY** 1 pilot, 6 passengers
- **WEAPONS** 6 solar ionisation panels, ion drive array

DARTH MAUL

CLOAKING DEVICE ALLOWS MAUL TO TRAVEL UNNOTICED

AUTO-BRAKE SYSTEM IF STEERING COLUMN IS RELEASED

LOW CENTER OF GRAVITY

WINGS FOLD UPON LANDING

SITH SPEEDER, *BLOODFIN*
- **SIZE** 1.65 m (5 ft 6 in) long
- **SPEED** 650 km/h (404 mph)
- **CAPACITY** 1 pilot
- **WEAPONS** None

Speeders and STARSHIPS

Whether they are tracking a nearby Jedi, travelling to a clandestine meeting or attacking a secret Rebel base, the Sith have many vehicles at their disposal. From one-person speeders and stealthy starships to enormous Imperial warships, each Sith selects his vehicle depending on his mission.

COMMUNICATIONS GRID

IMPERIAL SHUTTLE
- **SIZE** 20 m (66 ft) long
- **MAX ACCELERATION** 1,400 G
- **CAPACITY** 6 crew, 20 passengers
- **WEAPONS** 2 twin laser cannons, 1 twin blaster cannon

LOWER WINGS FOLD UP FOR LANDING

TIE FIGHTER HANGARS

DARTH SIDIOUS

GEONOSIAN SPEEDER
- **SIZE** 3.2 m (10 ft 7 in) long
- **SPEED** 634 km/h (394 mph)
- **CAPACITY** 1 pilot
- **WEAPONS** None

CAN CLIMB TO ALTITUDE OF 2 KM (1.2 MILES) HIGH

SOLAR SAILER
- **SIZE** 16.8 m (55 ft) long, 105.2 m (345 ft) with sail open
- **MAX ACCELERATION** 1,000 G
- **CAPACITY** 3 crew, 1 passenger
- **WEAPONS** 84 miniature tractor-repulsor projectors

DARTH TYRANUS

UNIQUE SAIL FROM GREE ENCLAVE

FLOWN BY FA-4 PILOT DROID

WHAT HONOUR IS THERE AMONG THE SITH?

THE SITH RELY ON deception to achieve their goals. They are willing to cheat, lie, corrupt and murder – and they cannot even trust each other. Darth Sidious understands the power of betrayal: by deceiving those around him, he rises to power. And by destroying his own apprentice, he finds a new, more powerful protégé.

PLAYING WITH LIVES

Darth Sidious feels no guilt for placing others in danger: he cares only for his own plans. When Sidious wants to judge whether Anakin is vulnerable to the dark side, he fakes his own kidnapping and calls the Jedi to his rescue. Anakin and Obi-Wan risk their lives, while Palpatine remains safe all along.

MINDLESS VIOLENCE

The Sith are willing to destroy innocent lives. Darth Vader and Grand Moff Tarkin assure Rebel leader Princess Leia that they will not destroy her home planet, Alderaan – but the Sith don't honor their promises. They proceed to test their new superweapon, the Death Star, on Alderaan, destroying the peaceful planet completely.

LACK OF LOYALTY

Darth Sidious shows no loyalty – even to his own apprentice, Darth Tyranus. Sidious instructs Anakin to destroy Tyranus, simply to see whether the young Jedi will obey. Anakin's obedience proves that he can be turned to the dark side.

SEPARATIST ARMY
Darth Tyranus, masquerading as Separatist leader Count Dooku, convinces Nute Gunray and Poggle the Lesser to built an enormous Droid Army in the factories of Geonosis.

POGGLE THE LESSER

The Separatist war room on the lava planet Mustafar is a flurry of military activity. Darth Sidious sends his orders via hologram, while Separatist officers and battle droids implement Droid Army strategy using control panels and long-distance comlinks.

ARCHDUKE
Poggle the Lesser is the Archduke of Geonosis and a senior member of the Separatist Council. Following his successful creation of the Droid Army, Poggle now commands hives of Geonosians in a top-secret project for Darth Tyranus.

.... COMMAND STAFF MADE FROM THE BONES OF A MURDERED POLITICAL OPPONENT

COLLECTION OF STOLEN LIGHTSABERS FROM JEDI VICTIMS IS CONCEALED WITHIN CLOAK

HUMAN ORGANS ENCASED IN ROBOTIC BODY

GENERAL GRIEVOUS

SUPREME COMMANDER
General Grievous was chosen to command the Droid Army because of his savage reputation. The cyborg's hatred for the Jedi is an added bonus.

Allies of the SITH

The Separatists want to break away from Republic rule. They have joined forces with the Sith and built a fearsome Droid Army. But in pursuit of independence, their aggressive and violent tactics quickly raise alarm.

SEPARATISTS
LEADER: COUNT DOOKU
ALLEGIANCE: SITH
HEADQUARTERS: RAXUS
WEAPONS: DROID ARMY
VALUES: INDEPENDENCE, MILITARY POWER

SITH STRATEGY:
CLONE WARS

Darth Sidious is secretly in control of both the Republic and the Separatists. He uses his powerful position to spark the Clone Wars, during which he plays both sides against each other, hoping to destroy all opposition and assume complete control of the galaxy. The Sith Lord carries out his Clone Wars battle plan, revelling in the chaos he creates.

1. BUILD A SECRET ARMY

OBJECTIVE:
Create an army for the Republic, which is secretly loyal to the Sith.

OUTCOME:
The Clone Army is deployed by the Republic. Jedi Generals fight alongside clone troopers, unaware of their true allegiance. MISSION COMPLETE.

2. GAIN TRUST OF THE JEDI

OBJECTIVE:
Palpatine to avoid suspicion and remain involved in the plans of the Jedi.

OUTCOME:
The Jedi trust Chancellor Palpatine and discuss political matters and military strategy with him. MISSION COMPLETE.

3. TAKE CONTROL OF CLONE ARMY

OBJECTIVE:
Darth Sidious to activate Order 66 and place the Clone Army under Sith control.

OUTCOME:
Order 66 initiated successfully, commanding clone troopers to destroy the Jedi. The resulting Jedi Purge wipes out almost every Jedi and Padawan. MISSION COMPLETE.

> " I have good news for you, my lord. **WAR HAS BEGUN.** "
>
> Darth Tyranus

4. DESTROY THE JEDI ORDER

OBJECTIVE:
Destroy the Jedi Order once and for all.
....

OUTCOME:
The Jedi Temple, home to the Jedi Order, is destroyed. The few surviving Jedi are forced to flee into exile. MISSION INCOMPLETE.

OBJECTIVE:
Destroy all obstacles to total control.
....

OUTCOME:
New apprentice Darth Vader sent to annihilate the Separatist Council. No governing body remains to oppose Sidious's takeover of the Senate and galaxy. MISSION COMPLETE.

5. OBLITERATE THE SEPARATISTS

6. RULE THE GALAXY

OBJECTIVE:
Sidious to become sole ruler of the galaxy.
....

OUTCOME:
Sidious blames a Jedi plot for the fall of the Republic. He declares that the Republic will become a Galactic Empire – and he will rule as Emperor. MISSION COMPLETE.

CONSEQUENCES:

The galaxy is plunged into darkness after the Clone Wars. With the surviving Jedi forced into exile, there is no stopping Sidious from assuming the role of Emperor. The Sith Lord now has total control of the galaxy.

WHAT HAPPENS WHEN THE SITH START A WAR?

AS THE CLONE WARS wreak terror and destruction across the galaxy, the Sith are happy to let others fight their battles. The Separatists' Droid Army sweeps over the plains of Geonosis, marking the start of a war that will engulf the galaxy and lead to the loss of thousands of lives.

JEDI GENERALS

As the Clone Wars begin, the Jedi lead the Clone Army in battle. Although the Jedi Order usually prefers negotiation to combat, the Clone Wars present them with a choice: fight to protect their values... or accept the actions of the Sith.

SITH COMMANDER

As they march across Geonosis, the soldiers and machines of the Droid Army receive orders from the Trade Federation. These orders, in turn, come from Darth Tyranus, their lord and master.

DESTRUCTION

The Clone Wars draw to a close following Order 66, and the Jedi must accept their defeat. The Sith have triumphed and Darth Sidious has turned the Republic into his Empire. As the Jedi Temple burns, the surviving Jedi go into hiding.

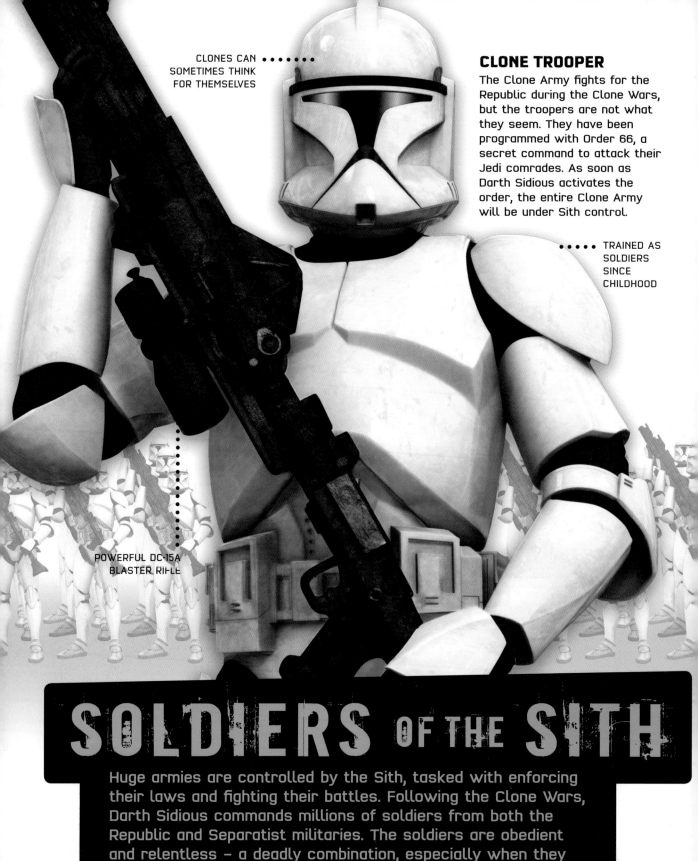

CLONES CAN SOMETIMES THINK FOR THEMSELVES

CLONE TROOPER

The Clone Army fights for the Republic during the Clone Wars, but the troopers are not what they seem. They have been programmed with Order 66, a secret command to attack their Jedi comrades. As soon as Darth Sidious activates the order, the entire Clone Army will be under Sith control.

TRAINED AS SOLDIERS SINCE CHILDHOOD

POWERFUL DC-15A BLASTER RIFLE

SOLDIERS OF THE SITH

Huge armies are controlled by the Sith, tasked with enforcing their laws and fighting their battles. Following the Clone Wars, Darth Sidious commands millions of soldiers from both the Republic and Separatist militaries. The soldiers are obedient and relentless – a deadly combination, especially when they are programmed to enforce the evil orders of the Sith.

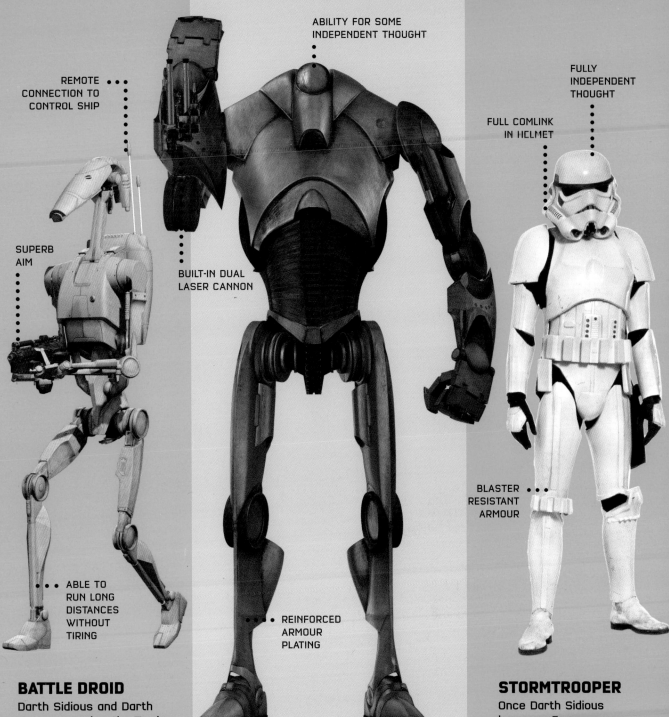

REMOTE
CONNECTION TO
CONTROL SHIP

ABILITY FOR SOME
INDEPENDENT THOUGHT

FULLY
INDEPENDENT
THOUGHT

FULL COMLINK
IN HELMET

SUPERB
AIM

BUILT-IN DUAL
LASER CANNON

BLASTER
RESISTANT
ARMOUR

ABLE TO
RUN LONG
DISTANCES
WITHOUT
TIRING

REINFORCED
ARMOUR
PLATING

BATTLE DROID

Darth Sidious and Darth
Tyranus employ the Trade
Federation to build an
enormous Droid Army.
Millions of battle droids
swarm across the galaxy
during the Clone Wars,
on a mission to defeat
the Republic.

SUPER BATTLE DROID

Super battle droids are upgraded droid
soldiers. They join regular battle droids
on the battlefield during the Clone
Wars, mindlessly obeying the orders
of their Sith-serving controllers.

STORMTROOPER

Once Darth Sidious
becomes Emperor,
he transforms the
Clone Army into the
mighty Imperial Army.
Stormtroopers patrol
every corner of the
galaxy, ensuring that
Sith law is obeyed
without question.

WHAT HAPPENS
WHEN A SITH IS EXPOSED?

DARTH SIDIOUS HAS been masquerading as Supreme Chancellor Palpatine for many years, but it is only a matter of time until his betrayal is discovered. When the Jedi realise that their nemesis is actually the Supreme Chancellor, Mace Windu leads a team of Jedi Masters to arrest the Sith Lord. The Jedi are armed with lightsabers, well aware that a Sith will not surrender quietly.

CONFRONTATION

Darth Sidious is quick to react when confronted. He reveals his hidden lightsaber and displays his deadly Sith powers by destroying Jedi Saesee Tiin, Agen Kolar and Kit Fisto in a matter of seconds.

ATTACK

Darth Sidious then turns his lightsaber on Mace Windu. But the Jedi demonstrates his deadly Vaapad combat skills and pushes Sidious to the brink of defeat.

CHOOSING SIDES

Mace is about to deal the fatal blow when Anakin Skywalker appears. Sidious seizes the opportunity to turn Anakin to the dark side once and for all: he pretends he is too weak to defend himself and begs Anakin to save him. Anakin makes a quick decision. He cuts off Mace's lightsaber hand, giving Sidious the chance to destroy Mace with Sith lightning.

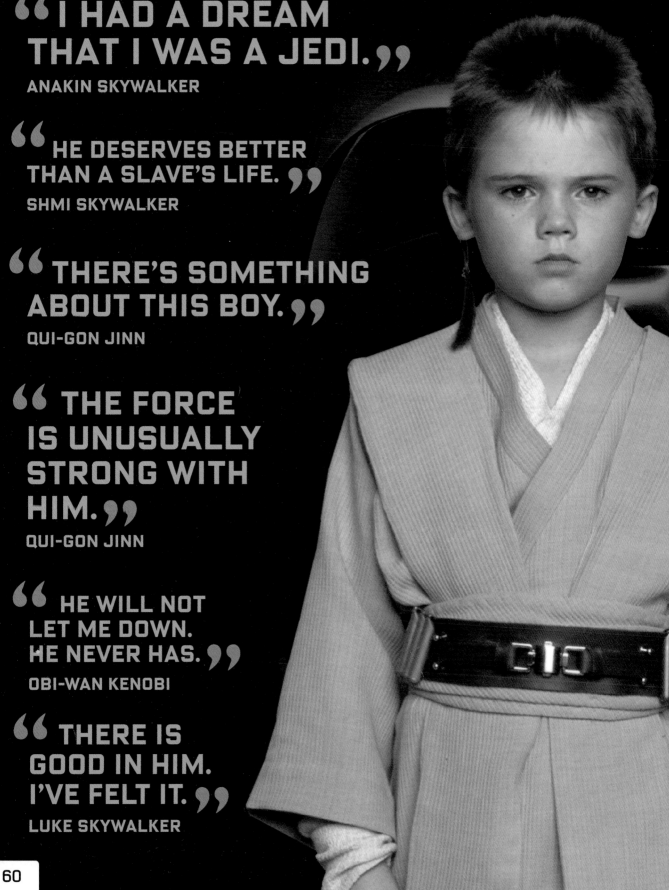

"I HAD A DREAM THAT I WAS A JEDI."
ANAKIN SKYWALKER

"HE DESERVES BETTER THAN A SLAVE'S LIFE."
SHMI SKYWALKER

"THERE'S SOMETHING ABOUT THIS BOY."
QUI-GON JINN

"THE FORCE IS UNUSUALLY STRONG WITH HIM."
QUI-GON JINN

"HE WILL NOT LET ME DOWN. HE NEVER HAS."
OBI-WAN KENOBI

"THERE IS GOOD IN HIM. I'VE FELT IT."
LUKE SKYWALKER

> ## "I'M NOT THE JEDI I SHOULD BE. I WANT MORE – BUT I KNOW I SHOULDN'T."
> **ANAKIN SKYWALKER**

> ## "I DON'T TRUST HIM."
> **MACE WINDU**

> ## "TWISTED BY THE DARK SIDE, YOUNG SKYWALKER HAS BECOME."
> **YODA**

> ## "THE BOY IS DANGEROUS."
> **OBI-WAN KENOBI**

> ## "THE FORCE IS STRONG WITH YOU! A POWERFUL SITH, YOU WILL BECOME."
> **DARTH SIDIOUS**

THE DARKNESS WITHIN

Anakin Skywalker was always expected to do great things. His connection with the Force meant that he became the greatest Jedi the galaxy had ever seen. Yet, even from a young age, Anakin's soul was in turmoil. He often wants more. Is his fall to the dark side inevitable?

Following a brutal duel against Obi-Wan Kenobi, Vader's human body was almost completely destroyed. Life-supporting armour now conceals all that remains of Anakin Skywalker.

BETRAYED BY EMOTION

Vader used to be Anakin Skywalker, a famous Jedi Knight, but he was never able to overcome his negative emotions. He feared the death of his wife, Padmé, and was turned to the dark side by Darth Sidious who exploited his feelings.

Darth VADER

Sith apprentice Darth Vader is the leader of the Imperial Army. He seeks to crush the Rebellion against his Master, the Emperor. Vader will not tolerate weakness and shows no mercy – even to his own troops.

SITH STATS

SPECIES: HUMAN
HOMEWORLD: TATOOINE
BIRTHDATE: 41 BBY
HEIGHT: 2.02 M (6 FT 8 IN)
TRAINED BY: DARTH SIDIOUS
WEAPONS: RED-BLADED LIGHTSABER
TRADEMARK: FORCE CHOKE

DURASTEEL ARMOUR
PROTECTS MOBILE
LIFE-SUPPORT SYSTEM

RESPIRATORY DEVICE
AMPLIFIES BREATHING
SOUNDS

FORCE CONNECTION

Darth Vader has strong
Force powers, which make
him an expert pilot and
lightsaber combatant. He
also uses the Force to sense
the feelings of those around
him, giving him a constant
advantage over others.

FATHER AND SON

Darth Vader senses many similarities between
himself and his son, Luke Skywalker. He tries
to convince Luke to become his Sith apprentice,
so father and son can overthrow the Emperor
and rule together.

CAN A SITH DEFEAT HIS FORMER JEDI MASTER?

WHEN A JEDI turns to the dark side, the Jedi Order is forever haunted by the loss. A fallen Jedi is a great threat because he knows the secrets of the Order and has been trained in the light side of the Force. So, when a fallen Jedi battles his former Jedi Master, their shared history can become a powerful weapon.

KNOW YOUR ENEMY

When Darth Tyranus faces Yoda on the planet Geonosis, the Sith uses his knowledge of Yoda's Jedi values to escape. He forces Yoda to make a choice: defeat Tyranus or save Anakin and Obi-Wan from being crushed.

LIGHT VS DARK

Yoda is troubled to learn that Count Dooku has chosen the dark side. He is determined to stop the former Jedi, no matter how powerful he has become.

OLD FRIENDS

On Mustafar, the newly created Sith Lord Darth Vader attacks his former friend and Jedi Master, Obi-Wan Kenobi. Vader calls on the dark side to harness more power, but he is overwhelmed by rage. Obi-Wan takes advantage of Darth Vader's weaknesses and defeats him.

SACRIFICE

Many years later, Obi-Wan and Darth Vader duel for a second time. The Sith Lord is now more experienced and powerful. However, the Jedi knows something that Vader does not – that there is life beyond death. Obi-Wan submits to Vader's death blow, so that Luke and the Rebels can escape – and that he may continue to teach Luke.

Rebellion
against the SITH

In a galaxy obedient to the Sith, few are brave enough to resist. The Rebel Alliance aims to restore the galaxy to its former state as a democratic Republic and to end the terrible dictatorship of the Sith and their Empire.

The Rebels are willing to die for their cause. They protect their Echo Base headquarters on Hoth against invading Imperial troops, even though they are vastly outnumbered.

REBEL WITH A CAUSE
Princess Leia Organa is the Empire's youngest and most determined Senator. She is on a mission to destroy the Death Star and the danger it poses.

THE LAST JEDI
Luke Skywalker is astonished to learn he has Force powers. He begins his Jedi training and joins the Rebel Alliance. Luke is determined to destroy the Sith and learn the truth about his father.

PRINCESS LEIA

REBEL ALLIANCE

LEADER: MON MOTHMA
ALLEGIANCE: REBEL ALLIANCE
HEADQUARTERS: *HOME ONE*
WEAPONS: DH-17 BLASTER PISTOL, A280 BLASTER RIFLF
VALUES: DEMOCRACY, FREEDOM

QUICK ON THE DRAW, HAN SOLO IS GOOD IN A DUEL

HONOURABLE SMUGGLER

Han Solo didn't intend to join the Rebel Alliance, but he proves an invaluable pilot when he chooses to join his friends in their fight against the Sith.

LUKE SKYWALKER

HAN SOLO

DL-44 BLASTER PISTOL

REBEL MIGHT

The Rebel Fleet is small but dangerous. Flying their one-seater B-wings, X-wings and Y-wings, Rebel pilots defeat the enormous ships of the Imperial Navy, thanks to careful planning, impressive skill and plenty of courage.

67

SUPERWEAPONS

The Force is more powerful than any weapon, but it can't be seen or touched. Darth Sidious wants to create a physical symbol of his immense power to strike fear into the hearts of everyone in the galaxy. The Sith Lord orders the construction of a huge, mobile battle station called the Death Star, which has enough firepower to destroy an entire planet. Even when the Death Star is destroyed by Rebel forces, Sidious uses the might and resources of the Empire to build a second, even more terrifying Death Star.

MAIN POWER GENERATOR

HYPERMATTER REACTOR

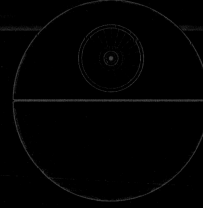

DEATH STAR I
- **SIZE** 160 km (99 miles) diameter
- **HYPERDRIVE RATING** Class 4.0
- **MAXIMUM SPEED** 10 MGLT
- **SUPERLASER RECHARGE** 24 hours
- **COMBAT VEHICLES** 11,000
- **PERSONNEL** 1.7 million

DEATH STAR II
- **SIZE** 900 km (550 miles) diameter
- **HYPERDRIVE RATING** Class 3.0
- **MAXIMUM SPEED** 20 MGLT
- **SUPERLASER RECHARGE** 3 minutes
- **COMBAT VEHICLES** 25,000
- **PERSONNEL** 2.5 million

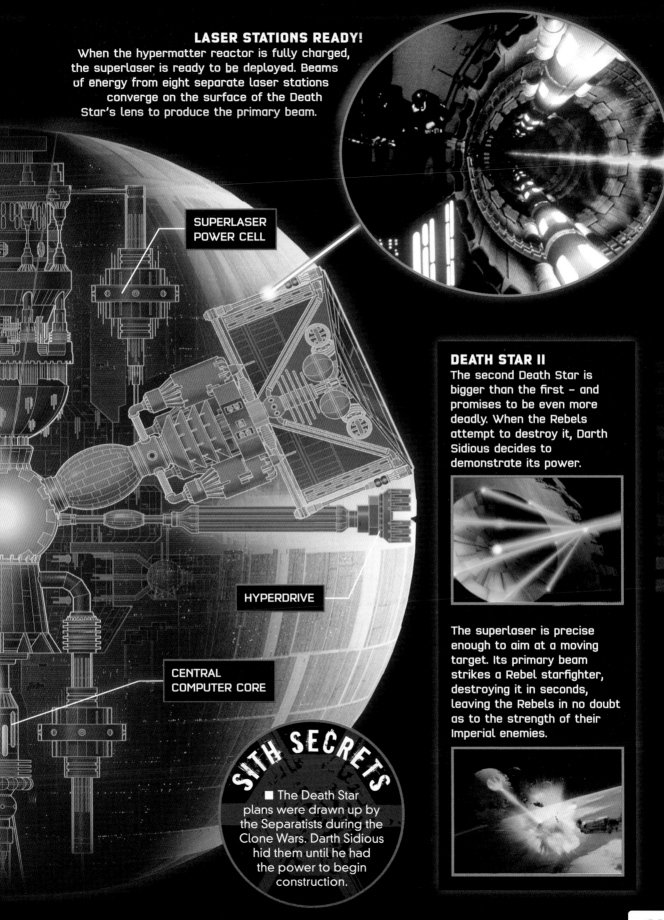

LASER STATIONS READY!

When the hypermatter reactor is fully charged, the superlaser is ready to be deployed. Beams of energy from eight separate laser stations converge on the surface of the Death Star's lens to produce the primary beam.

SUPERLASER POWER CELL

HYPERDRIVE

CENTRAL COMPUTER CORE

SITH SECRETS

■ The Death Star plans were drawn up by the Separatists during the Clone Wars. Darth Sidious hid them until he had the power to begin construction.

DEATH STAR II

The second Death Star is bigger than the first – and promises to be even more deadly. When the Rebels attempt to destroy it, Darth Sidious decides to demonstrate its power.

The superlaser is precise enough to aim at a moving target. Its primary beam strikes a Rebel starfighter, destroying it in seconds, leaving the Rebels in no doubt as to the strength of their Imperial enemies.

A SITH AMONG THEM
Most Imperial soldiers remain unaware that the Emperor is a Sith Lord. Darth Sidious is rarely seen by the Imperial troops, although he often sends his apprentice Darth Vader to inspect the progress of his military projects.

OFFICER'S DISC

IMPERIAL CODE CYLINDER

LIEUTENANT SHECKIL

FEAR OF FAILURE
During a mission to Cloud City, Lieutenant Sheckil is Darth Vader's second-in-command. When Sheckil fails to complete his assignment, he worries that he might have to face the legendary wrath of Darth Vader.

SECRET DATA STORED IN BELT BUCKLE DISC

Even small, out-of-the-way planets like Tatooine must submit to Imperial patrols. Sandtroopers search the desert on dewback mounts, keeping an eye out for their quarry.

IMPERIAL ARMY

LEADER: EMPEROR PALPATINE
ALLEGIANCE: EMPIRE
HEADQUARTERS: CORUSCANT
WEAPONS: E-11 BLASTER RIFLE, THERMAL DETONATOR
VALUES: IMPERIAL LAW, OBEDIENCE

Army OF THE EMPIRE

The Imperial military has a fearsome reputation. Charged with enforcing Emperor Palpatine's laws, armour-clad stormtroopers patrol the far reaches of the galaxy. As Emperor, Darth Sidious issues orders from his Throne Room, intent on destroying the Rebellion.

INTERROGATION DROID

IT-O

Just one look at this fearsome hovering droid is usually enough to make prisoners talk. The IT-O contains many dangerous tools and deadly functions that are designed to scare prisoners into revealing any hidden secrets to their captors.

PROTOCOL DROID

RA-7

Built to serve high-ranking Imperial officers, this protocol droid is also equipped with a secret surveillance system, so he can spy on his surroundings.

MOUSE DROID

MSE-6

These droids are used exclusively by the Imperial Navy. They perform simple tasks, such as delivering messages and escorting troops around the Death Star.

ASTROMECH DROID

R2-Q5

Stationed on the second Death Star, R2-Q5 performs normal astromech duties such as repairing starships, but he is also equipped with hidden spy devices.

Sith DROIDS

Droids are used across the galaxy for many purposes. The Sith often have unique requirements for their droids, so they have been known to commission their own designs, or update already existing models to use for their wicked purposes.

DRK-1

Darth Maul's Dark Eye probe droid was designed using plans from a Sith Holocron. It features a long-distance transmission antenna and a stealth mechanism that enables it to avoid detection.

VIPER PROBE

Sent across the galaxy to track targets for the Imperial Army, the Viper probe droid is a less specialised model than the Dark Eye. It is equipped with weapons and a self-destruct device.

MEDICAL DROIDS

TRIPEDAL MEDDROIDS

Designed by Darth Sidious, these three-legged assistant droids have specially designed arms that can operate with incredible precision.

FX-6

This medical assistant droid helps repair Darth Vader's body after his duel with Obi-Wan on Mustafar. He has seven multi-functional upper arms and 13 lower arms, as well as many vials of medical fluids, such as bacta.

NOWHERE TO HIDE
The Sith extend their influence by deploying Imperial commanders and their troops to thousands of distant planets. Carrying out Sith orders and policing galactic citizens, the stormtroopers are feared as an extension of their power. Few people dare to disobey.

HOW DO THE SITH MAINTAIN CONTROL?

THERE ARE ONLY EVER two Sith, so to control an entire galaxy, they must use all their cunning. By crafting a terrifying reputation, the Sith use fear to keep order. They shroud themselves in mystery and encourage rumours that inspire dread in all who hear them. The Sith ensure everyone knows that they don't tolerate weakness. They don't forgive and they never forget.

UNFORGIVING
Darth Vader instills terror in his own troops to keep them under control. His punishment for an officer's mistake is death by Force choke.

SHROUDED IN SECRECY
Darth Sidious establishes a fearsome reputation among his own officers, even Darth Vader. He keeps his visits to the Death Star to a minimum, so that when he does appear – half-concealed by his black cloak – he is surrounded by an air of awe and terror. Imperial officers are terrified of his wrath.

FACE CLOTH TO MASK ZAM'S FACE

BLENDING IN

Zam Wesell is a shapeshifting assassin, hired to destroy Padmé Amidala. Before Zam can complete her mission, she is caught by two Jedi Knights. About to identify her client, Zam is silenced with a saberdart – fired by bounty hunter Jango Fett.

SPECIAL FABRIC ALLOWS ZAM TO BLEND INTO SHADOWS

COMLINK

HIRED HELP

LEADER: NONE
ALLEGIANCE: WHOEVER OFFERS THE HIGHEST PRICE
WEAPONS: E-11 BLASTER RIFLE, THERMAL DETONATOR
VALUES: JOB COMPLETION, MONEY, BLASTER SKILLS

JETPACK CONTAINS ROCKET LAUNCHER

DENGAR
Remorseless killer

ZAM WESELL

RUTHLESS

Jango Fett is a superb marksman – and a top fighter even without his blaster. His tough armour and diverse collection of weaponry means you definitely don't want him on your trail!

JANGO FETT

JANGO FETT'S DNA IS USED TO CREATE THE CLONE ARMY

A BARGAIN WITH THE SITH

The Sith are powerful enough to force others to obey them. When Darth Vader tracks the Rebels to Cloud City, he makes a deal with Baron Administrator Lando Calrissian. If Lando hands over the Rebels, Cloud City will remain free from Imperial control. Lando agrees, although he later has second thoughts about aiding the Sith.

BOBA FETT
Deadly
marksman

BOSSK
Vengeful
hunter

ZUCKUSS
Relentless
tracker

4-LOM
Criminal
droid

Darth Vader is desperate to catch a small group of Rebels, so he employs the services of some of the most famous bounty hunters in the galaxy: Dengar, IG-88, Boba Fett, Bossk, 4-LOM and Zuckuss.

Bounty HUNTERS

Sith Lords prefer to control events from a safe distance and often hire others to do their work for them. To carry out dangerous tasks, such as catching their enemies, the Sith often turn to bounty hunters and assassins, who will take on any mission – no matter how evil – for a fee.

HOW POWERFUL IS A CYBORG HIRED BY THE SITH?

SUPREME COMMANDER of the Separatist Droid Army, General Grievous wields much power. His cyborg body is fast and strong, and he is fueled by a deep hatred of the Jedi. With the might of the Droid Army behind him, his ability to wield four lightsabers at once and his renowned tactical skills, Grievous is one opponent who must not be underestimated.

BODY ARMOUR

Injured by a bomb, General Grievous's living body was almost destroyed. His remains were built into a duranium shell, turning him into a cyborg. Now, Grievous's tough, metal body is one of his greatest strengths. The cyborg is able to withstand the crushing pressures of outer space when he escapes from the Jedi through the window of his starship, *Invisible Hand*.

NO MATCH FOR A JEDI
Although the fearsome cyborg has been trained in the art of lightsaber combat by Darth Tyranus, he cannot fully harness the power of the dark side. When Grievous finally comes face to face with Obi-Wan Kenobi, he cannot match the Jedi's skills and is soon defeated.

SITH TARGET:
LUKE SKYWALKER

When Darth Vader discovers the existence of his son, Luke Skywalker, he embarks on a mission to recruit Luke to the dark side. Luke has begun his Jedi training, so Vader will need all his cunning and skill to turn his son into a Sith. Fortunately for Vader, he has all the resources of the Empire at his disposal...

1. LOCATE LUKE SKYWALKER

OBJECTIVE:
Imperial Army to discover the location of Rebel headquarters and capture Luke Skywalker.

OUTCOME:
Probe droids locate Echo Base headquarters on Hoth, but Luke and the Rebels escape.
MISSION INCOMPLETE.

2. THE LURE

OBJECTIVE:
Darth Vader to lure Luke to Cloud City by capturing his friends, Princess Leia and Han Solo.

OUTCOME:
Han Solo is frozen in carbonite and the others are captured. Luke arrives to rescue his friends, but is confronted by Vader.
MISSION COMPLETE.

"Join me, and **TOGETHER** we can rule the galaxy as **FATHER AND SON**."

DARTH VADER

3. FIRST DUEL

OBJECTIVE:
Darth Vader to persuade Luke to become his Sith apprentice.

OUTCOME:
During a lightsaber duel, Vader reveals he is Luke's father. Luke refuses to join the dark side. MISSION FAILED.

4. THE POWER OF PERSUASION

OBJECTIVE:
Darth Vader to convince Luke to join forces with the Sith.

OUTCOME:
Luke comes to the Death Star voluntarily, but Vader is unable to persuade him to join the Sith. MISSION FAILED.

5. THREATEN FRIENDS

OBJECTIVE:
Force Luke to join the dark side in order to protect his allies.

OUTCOME:
Luke's friends are captured and threatened, but Luke has faith in the Rebels' mission and refuses to join the dark side. MISSION FAILED.

6. FINAL DUEL

CONSEQUENCES:

Darth Vader fails at almost every stage of his plan. Luke not only proves his dedication to the Jedi Order, but also manages to awaken the last remnants of his father Anakin Skywalker's humanity. Father and son are at last reunited – on the light side of the Force.

OBJECTIVE:
Vader to turn Luke to the dark side – or destroy him.

OUTCOME:
Following a fierce duel with Vader, Luke is almost killed by the Emperor. But Vader finally returns to the light side and saves his son. MISSION FAILED.

WHO WILL TRIUMPH WHEN A SITH DUELS HIS SON?

SITH AND JEDI WARRIORS have dueled many times over the centuries. But this time the fate of the galaxy hangs not just on a battle between the dark side and the light side – but on a battle between father and son. Although Darth Vader and Luke Skywalker are equally strong in the Force, their duels are more than just about physical strength. Strong emotions influence their battles, but whose will is stronger?

A SON'S ANGER
When Darth Vader first duels Luke, he senses much of himself in the young Jedi. He encourages Luke to release his anger in an effort to turn him to the dark side.

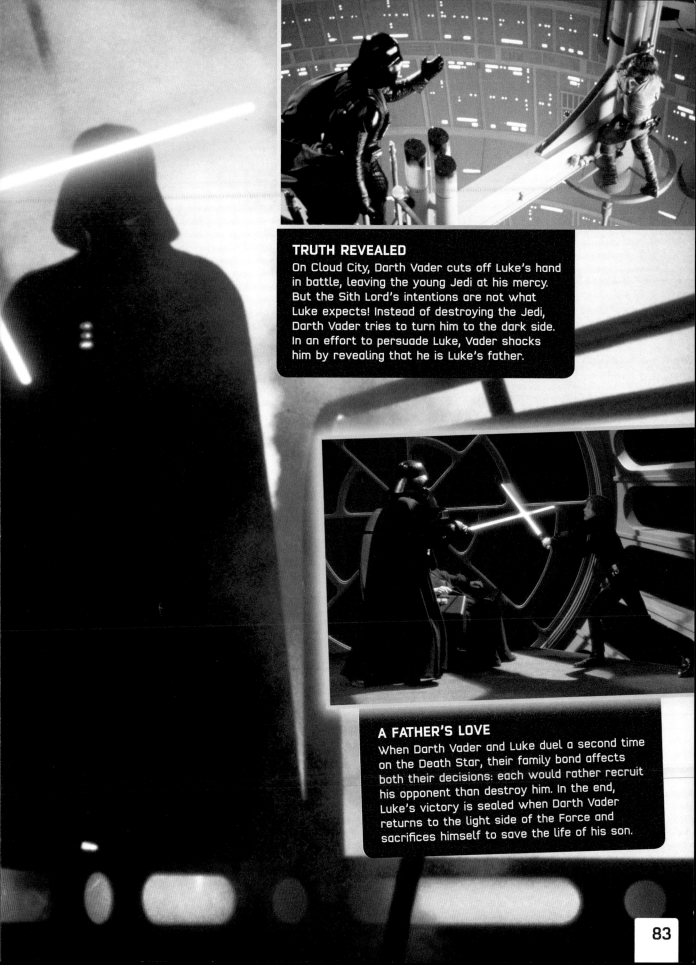

TRUTH REVEALED

On Cloud City, Darth Vader cuts off Luke's hand in battle, leaving the young Jedi at his mercy. But the Sith Lord's intentions are not what Luke expects! Instead of destroying the Jedi, Darth Vader tries to turn him to the dark side. In an effort to persuade Luke, Vader shocks him by revealing that he is Luke's father.

A FATHER'S LOVE

When Darth Vader and Luke duel a second time on the Death Star, their family bond affects both their decisions: each would rather recruit his opponent than destroy him. In the end, Luke's victory is sealed when Darth Vader returns to the light side of the Force and sacrifices himself to save the life of his son.

LIKE FATHER

In many ways, Jedi Luke Skywalker's life seems to be following a similar path to his father's. Although he never met the Jedi Anakin Skywalker, they have much in common. Can Luke use the light side of the Force to break the pattern and choose his own future? Only time will tell...

LATECOMER TO THE JEDI ORDER

Nine-year-old Anakin is a lot older than most younglings who begin their Jedi training. His special connection with the Force convinces the Jedi Order to train him.

Luke is 22 years old when he begins his Jedi training. No new Jedi have been trained since the Jedi Purge, but Yoda realises that Luke offers new hope for the exiled Jedi Order.

EXCEPTIONALLY STRONG IN THE FORCE

Anakin's Force skills enable him to pilot his spaceship at incredible speeds. He is one of the most famous pilots in the Republic.

Luke uses his sharp Jedi reflexes to pilot his spaceship with skill. His connection with the Force enables him to destroy the Death Star.

LIKE SON

I AM A JEDI, LIKE MY FATHER BEFORE ME."

LUKE SKYWALKER

HAUNTED BY VISIONS

Anakin is haunted by nightmares and fears for the people he loves. He grows less and less able to control these emotions.

Luke's feelings cause him to have dark side visions during his Jedi training. He must overcome these thoughts if he wants to progress.

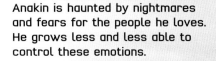
DISOBEDIENT

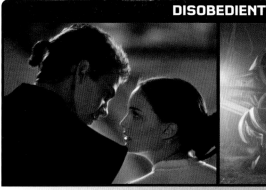

Anakin is a disobedient Padawan. He ignores many teachings of the Jedi Order, including the rule that a Jedi must not fall in love.

Luke refuses to heed Yoda's advice that he should complete his Jedi training. He rushes off to Cloud City, even though it is a trap.

SCARRED IN BATTLE

Anakin loses his right hand during a duel with Darth Tyranus. His injury serves as a reminder of his impatience and inexperience.

Luke's right hand is cut off by Darth Vader during their first duel. For Luke, the injury symbolises his similarities to his father.

Luke does not try to escape his destiny. He knows that his life is interlinked with his father's. But instead of accepting his fate and joining the Sith, Luke chooses to use his connection with Darth Vader to bring his father back to the light side of the Force.

ARE YOU
ABLE TO
CONTROL YOUR
EMOTIONS?

YES

IS FRIENDSHIP
MORE
IMPORTANT
THAN SUCCESS?

ARE YOU ON
A PATH TO THE
DARK SIDE?

NO

NO

Every decision has a consequence. Qui-Gon agreed to train Anakin as a Jedi. Anakin gave in to his anger and destroyed Darth Tyranus. Mace Windu believed Anakin was loyal to the Jedi Order. Luke refused to give up faith in his father. A single moment is all it takes to choose between the light side and the dark side. Now, the choice is yours: which path will you take?

IS STRENGTH
BETTER THAN
INTELLIGENCE?

NO

WOULD YOU
TRY TO NEGOTIATE
BEFORE ENTERING
A BATTLE?

NO

YES

DO YOU EVER
GO BACK ON
YOUR WORD?

YES

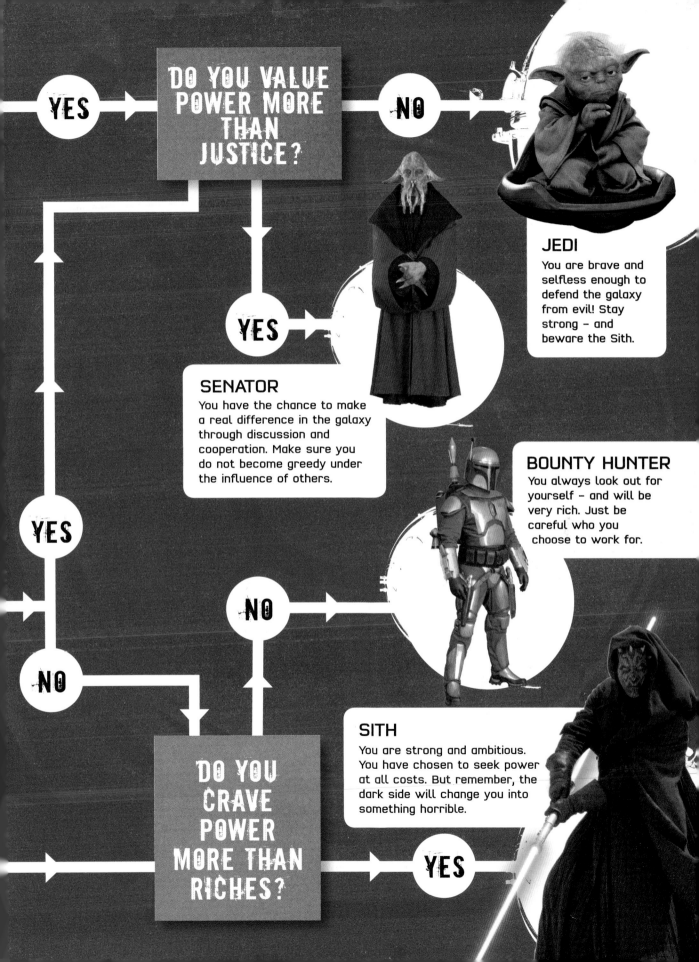

YES → **DO YOU VALUE POWER MORE THAN JUSTICE?** → NO

JEDI
You are brave and selfless enough to defend the galaxy from evil! Stay strong – and beware the Sith.

YES →

SENATOR
You have the chance to make a real difference in the galaxy through discussion and cooperation. Make sure you do not become greedy under the influence of others.

BOUNTY HUNTER
You always look out for yourself – and will be very rich. Just be careful who you choose to work for.

YES

NO → NO →

SITH
You are strong and ambitious. You have chosen to seek power at all costs. But remember, the dark side will change you into something horrible.

DO YOU CRAVE POWER MORE THAN RICHES? → YES

HOW CAN A SITH LORD BRING BALANCE TO THE FORCE?

DARTH VADER HAS spent years trying to turn his son Luke Skywalker to the dark side. When he finally escorts a willing Luke to the Emperor's Throne Room, it seems the Sith Lord has succeeded. However, when Luke bravely resists the Emperor and faces his wrath, Darth Vader begins to question his own allegiance to the Sith.

FAITH IN HIS FATHER

When Luke refuses to join the dark side, the Emperor attacks him with deadly Sith lightning. In agony, Luke calls out to Darth Vader, begging for help. After all these years, Luke still believes there is good in his father.

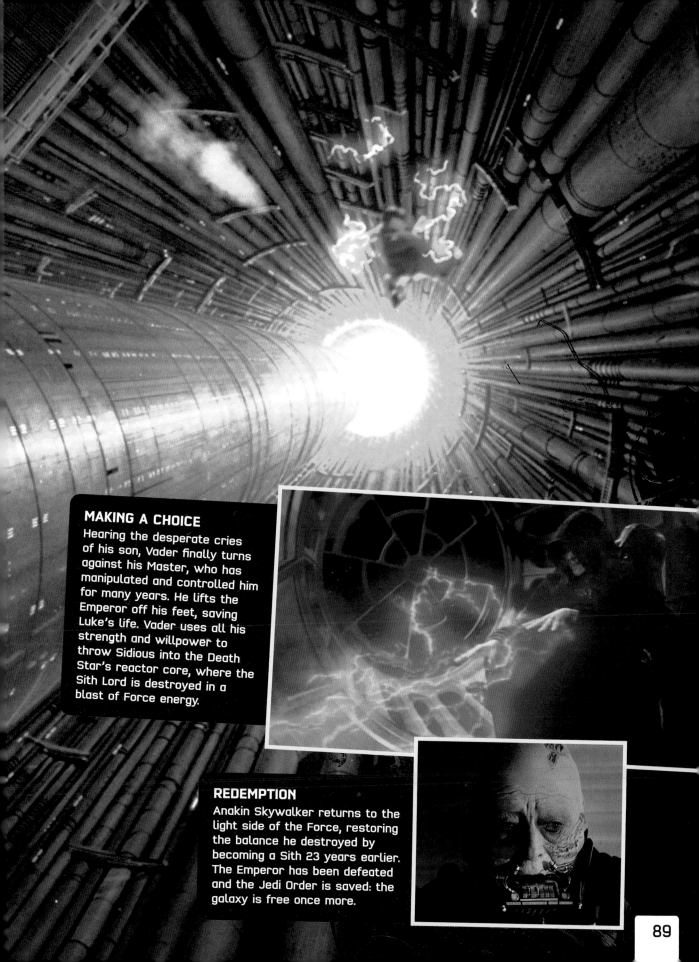

MAKING A CHOICE

Hearing the desperate cries of his son, Vader finally turns against his Master, who has manipulated and controlled him for many years. He lifts the Emperor off his feet, saving Luke's life. Vader uses all his strength and willpower to throw Sidious into the Death Star's reactor core, where the Sith Lord is destroyed in a blast of Force energy.

REDEMPTION

Anakin Skywalker returns to the light side of the Force, restoring the balance he destroyed by becoming a Sith 23 years earlier. The Emperor has been defeated and the Jedi Order is saved: the galaxy is free once more.

THE END OF THE SITH

When Anakin destroys Darth Sidious and returns to the light side of the Force, the Sith are finally destroyed. Although Anakin will not survive, he has succeeded in bringing balance to the Force... for now.

IS THIS THE END?

Darth Vader has once again become Anakin Skywalker. Emperor Palpatine has been destroyed. The Death Star has exploded into a billion pieces. As citizens of the galaxy celebrate and the Rebels and Jedi heroes reunite, it looks as if the Sith have been defeated once and for all. But the Sith are known to be sneaky. They survived undetected for over 1,000 years. Are they really gone for good?

SURVIVAL OF THE JEDI ORDER

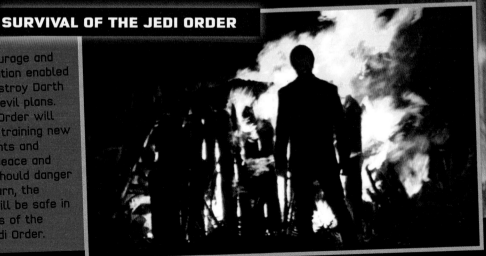

Luke's courage and determination enabled him to destroy Darth Sidious's evil plans. The Jedi Order will continue, training new Jedi Knights and seeking peace and justice. Should danger ever return, the galaxy will be safe in the hands of the noble Jedi Order.

AT ONE WITH THE FORCE

Anakin joins Yoda and Obi-Wan Kenobi as Force spirits. Their life energies are able to survive after death, living on through the Force to offer guidance to future Jedi.

FREEDOM FOR THE GALAXY

With the collapse of the feared Empire, the galaxy is free once more. Almost every planet celebrates the victory, thankful they are no longer living under the Emperor's rule.

GLOSSARY

ALDERAAN
■ A peaceful planet, known for its beauty and culture, located in the Core Worlds.

ASTROMECH DROID
■ A utility robot that repairs and helps navigate starships.

BATTLE OF YAVIN
■ Conflict in Year 0 where Rebel forces, based on the moon Yavin 4, attacked and destroyed the first Imperial Death Star.

BOUNTY HUNTER
■ Someone who tracks down, captures or kills wanted people in exchange for money.

CHANCELLOR
■ The title given to the head of the Galactic Senate and Republic.

CLONE ARMY
■ An army of genetically identical soldiers, all trained to be perfect warriors. They fight for the Republic.

CLONE WARS
■ A series of galaxy-wide battles fought between the Republic's Clone Army and the Droid Army of the Separatists, which took place between 22–19 BBY.

CORUSCANT
■ The capital of the Republic. This planet is home to the Senate building, the Jedi Temple and the Jedi Council.

CYBORG
■ A being that is partly a living organism and partly a robot.

DARK SIDE
■ The evil side of the Force that feeds off negative emotions and offers raw power to those who study it.

DEATH STAR
■ A planet-sized Imperial battle station, which has enough firepower to destroy an entire planet.

DEMOCRACY
■ A system of government where all senior politicians are elected by the population.

DICTATORSHIP
■ An oppressive government whose leader wants complete control over everyone.

EMPEROR
■ Ruler of the Empire.

EMPIRE
■ An oppressive power that ruled the galaxy from 19 BBY to 4 ABY under the leadership of Emperor Palpatine, a Sith Lord.

FORCE
■ The energy that flows through all living things, which can be used for either good or evil.

GEONOSIS
■ A rocky, desert planet in the Outer Rim Territories, famous for its droid factories.

HOLOCRON
■ An ancient device, activated through use of the Force, that contains large amounts of data.

HOTH
■ An ice-covered planet located in a remote sector of the Outer Rim Territories.

JEDI
■ A member of the Jedi Order who studies the light side of the Force.

JEDI COUNCIL
■ The 12 senior, respected members of the Jedi Order who meet to make important decisions and give advice.

JEDI KNIGHT

■ A member of the Jedi Order who has studied as a Padawan under a Jedi Master and who has passed the Jedi Trials.

JEDI MASTER

■ A rank for Jedi Knights who have performed an exceptional deed or have trained a Jedi Knight.

JEDI ORDER

■ An ancient organisation that promotes peace and justice throughout the galaxy.

JEDI PURGE

■ The attempt by Chancellor Palpatine in 19 BBY to annihilate the entire Jedi Order.

JEDI TEMPLE

■ The headquarters of the Jedi Order, located on the planet Coruscant.

LIGHTSABER

■ A weapon with a blade of pure energy that is used by Jedi and Sith warriors.

MUSTAFAR

■ A volcanic planet in the Outer Rim Territories, home to the Separatist Council at the end of the Clone Wars.

NABOO

■ A beautiful planet near the border of the Outer Rim Territories.

NEIMOIDIAN

■ A humanoid species native to the planet Neimoidia.

ORDER 66

■ An order given by Chancellor Palpatine that began the Jedi Purge. Every clone trooper in the Clone Army was ordered to kill all members of the Jedi Order.

PADAWAN

■ A Youngling who is chosen to serve an apprenticeship with a Jedi Master.

PROBE DROID

■ Imperial robot that gathers and transmits data.

REBEL ALLIANCE

■ The organisation that resists and fights against the Empire.

REPUBLIC

■ The democratic government of the galaxy, under leadership of an elected Chancellor.

SENATE

■ Government of the Republic, with representatives from all parts of the galaxy.

SENATOR

■ A person who represents their planet, sector or system in the Senate.

SEPARATISTS

■ An alliance against the Republic. Also known as the Confederacy of Independent Systems.

SITH APPRENTICE

■ A member of the Sith Order who has been selected for training by a Sith Master.

SITH LIGHTNING

■ Deadly rays of blue energy that can be used as a weapon by someone who has embraced the dark side of the Force.

SITH ORDER

■ An ancient sect of Force-sensitives who study the dark side to gain control and succeed in their greedy plans.

SITH CODE

■ A set of values and ancient teachings that guide the decisions of the members of the Sith Order.

SITH MASTER

■ A member of the Sith Order who passes on his knowledge of the dark side to an apprentice.

TATOOINE

■ A desert planet with two suns located in the Outer Rim Territories. Known as a meeting place for criminals and smugglers.

TRADE FEDERATION

■ A bureaucratic organisation that controls much of the trade and commerce in the galaxy.

YOUNGLING

■ A Force-sensitive child who joins the Jedi Order to be trained in the Jedi arts.

INDEX

Characters are listed under their most frequently used common name, for example Luke Skywalker is found under "L" and "Darth Tyranus" is under "D."

Main entries are in bold.

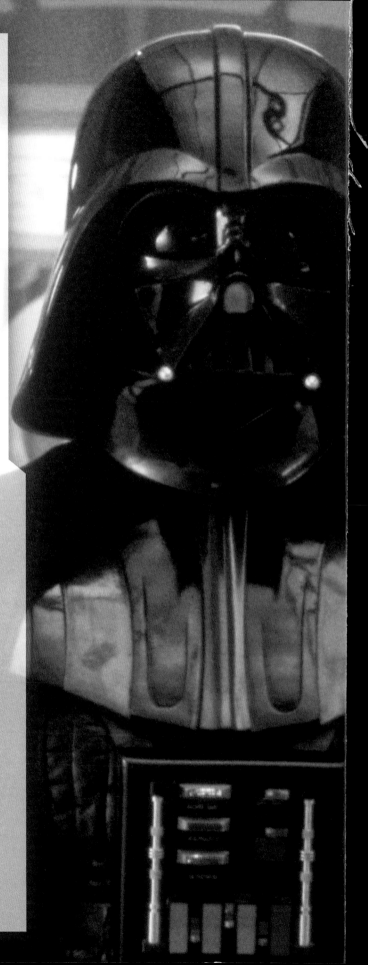

LONDON, NEW YORK, MELBOURNE,
MUNICH AND DELHI

For Dorling Kindersley

Editor Shari Last
Additional Editors Julia March, Helen Murray
Designers Clive Savage, Toby Truphet
Additional design by Lynne Moulding, Rhys Thomas
Design Manager Ron Stobbart
Art Director Lisa Lanzarini
Publishing Manager Catherine Saunders
Publisher Simon Beecroft
Publishing Director Alex Allan
Production Editor Siu Yin Chan
Production Controllers Man Fai Lau, Nick Seston

For Lucasfilm
Executive Editor J. W. Rinzler
Art Director Troy Alders
Keeper of the Holocron Leland Chee
Director of Publishing Carol Roeder

First published in Great Britain in 2012
by Dorling Kindersley Limited, 80 Strand, London WC2R ORL

10 9 8 7 6 5 4 3 2 1
001–182948—Mar/12

A CIP catalogue record for this book
is available from the British Library.

ISBN: 978-1-40539-140-5

Colour reproduction by Media Development Printing Ltd, UK.
Printed and bound in China by Hung Hing.

The publisher would like to thank Neil Ellis
for his artwork on pages 42–43 and Alastair
Dougall for his editorial assistance.

Discover more at
www.dk.com
www.starwars.com